Creepy Crawlies

Beetles

Rebecca Rissman

Raintree

www.raintreepublishers.co.uk
Visit our website to find out more information about Raintree books.

To order:
☎ Phone 0845 6044371
🗎 Fax +44 (0) 1865 312263
🖥 Email myorders@raintreepublishers.co.uk

Customers from outside the UK please telephone +44 1865 312262

Raintree is an imprint of Capstone Global Library Limited, a company incorporated in England and Wales having its registered office at 7 Pilgrim Street, London, EC4V 6LB – Registered company number: 6695582

Text © Capstone Global Library Limited 2013
First published in hardback in 2013
Paperback edition first published in 2014
The moral rights of the proprietor have been asserted.

Edited by Dan Nunn, Rebecca Rissman, and Catherine Veitch
Designed by Joanna Hinton-Malivoire
Picture research by Mica Brancic
Originated by Capstone Global Library Ltd
Production by Victoria Fitzgerald
Printed in China by South China Printing Company Ltd

ISBN 978 1 406 24132 7 (hardback)
16 15 14 13 12
10 9 8 7 6 5 4 3 2 1

ISBN 978 1 406 24146 4 (paperback)
17 16 15 14 13
10 9 8 7 6 5 4 3 2 1

British Library Cataloguing in Publication Data
Rissman, Rebecca.
Beetles. – (Creepy crawlies)
595.7'6-dc22
A full catalogue record for this book is available from the British Library.

Acknowledgements
We would like to thank the following for permission to reproduce photographs: Dreamstime pp. 13 (© Alslutsky), 22 (© Aetmeister); iStockphoto pp. 12, 23 (© Dimitris Stephanides), 19 (© Jim Jurica), 7 (© defun); Shutterstock pp. 4, 22 (© de2marco), 5, 22 (© Seiyoh), 5, 23 (© D. Kucharski & K. Kucharska), 8 (© Alslutsky, © Jamie Wilson, Steve Smith Photography), 8, 1 (© Adrov Andriy), 9a (© Alslutsky), 9b (© Cosmin Manci), 9c (© MilousSK), 11 (© Yuri Tuchkov), 15, 23 (© Cosmin Manci), 16 (© Yellowj), 18 (© Ortodox), 20 (© Eric Isselée), 21 (© Tyler Fox), 22 (© Alex Staroseltsev, © Péter Gudella, © Photolinc), 23 (© Anest, © Irin-k).

Cover photograph of a green beetle reproduced with permission of Shutterstock (© Igor Gorelchenkov).

Every effort has been made to contact copyright holders of any material reproduced in this book. Any omissions will be rectified in subsequent printings if notice is given to the publisher.

The publishers would like to thank Michael Bright for his assistance in the preparation of this book.

Contents

Let's search!

Do you see that insect
crawling on the ground?

It's a shiny beetle!
Look at what we've found.

5

What about this green beetle?
Can you see it over there?

Its wings are strong and shiny,
to keep it in the air.

wings

Are all beetles the same colour?
What colours have you seen?

Some are black, or red, or blue,
and some are even green!

Look at this black beetle.
It's swimming in a puddle.

Can you see its trail of
tiny floating bubbles?

11

Beetles can be different,
but some things are always true.

Beetles have six legs.
And antennae? They have two!

antennae

How many body parts do beetles have? How many can you see?

Let's count the beetle parts together: 1, 2, 3!

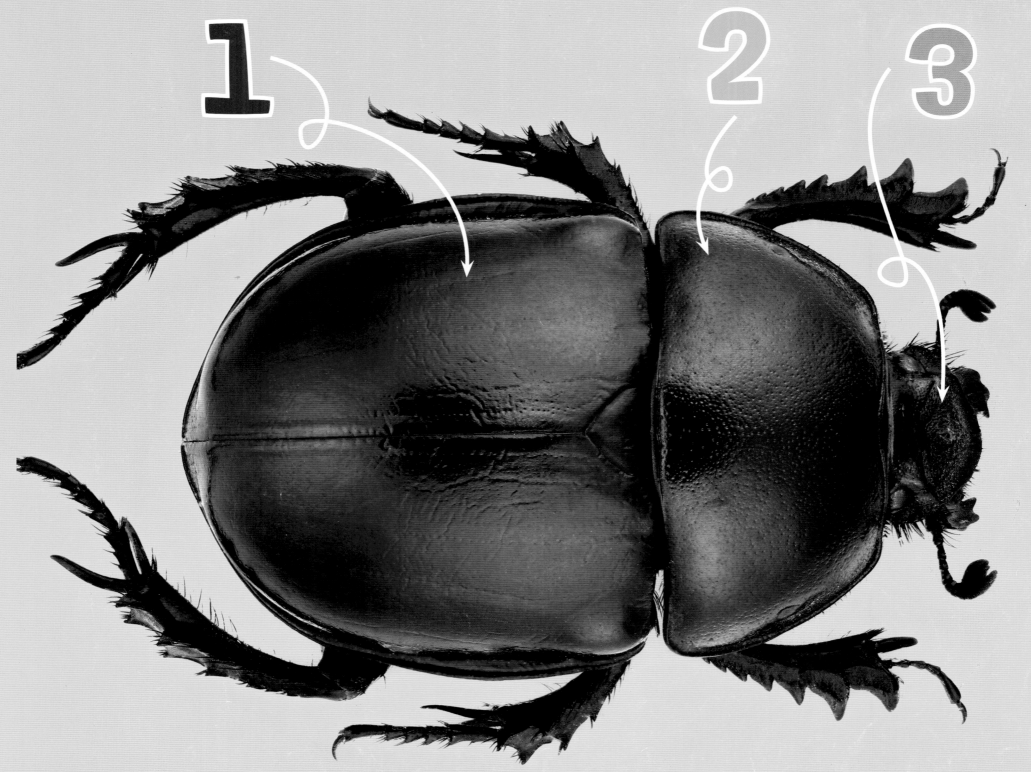

Where can you find beetles?
Look up, down, here, and there.

Beetles are clever bugs.
They can live almost anywhere!

Baby beetles, called larvae, don't look like their dad or mum.

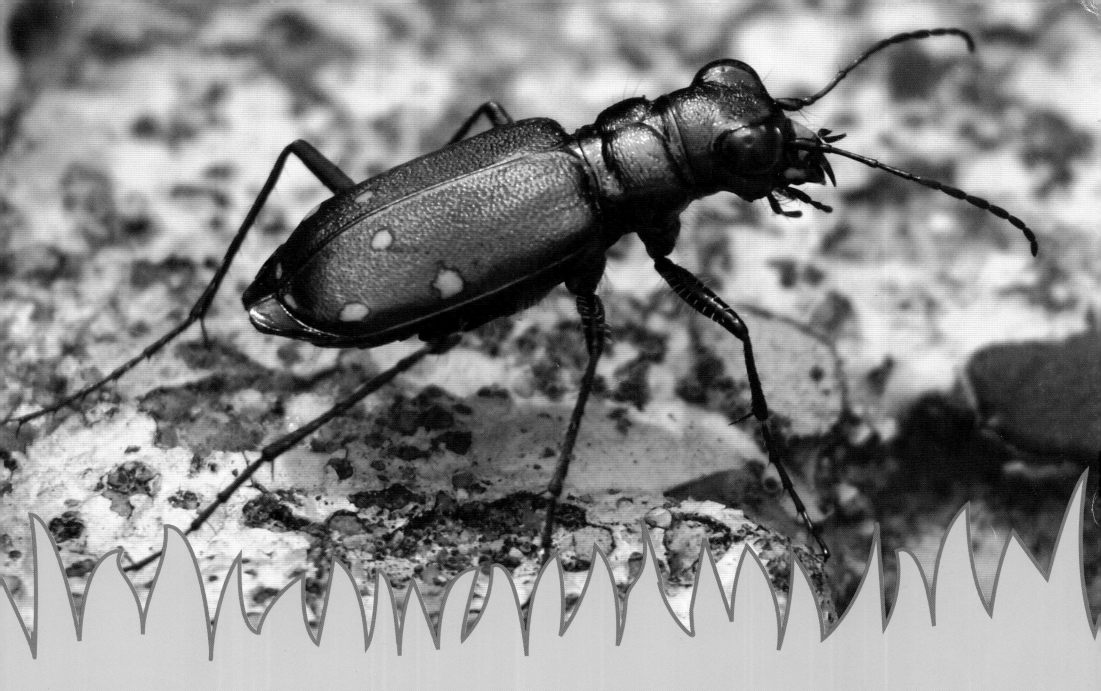

But beetles look more like their parents the older they become!

What do beetles eat, when they're crawling through the weeds?

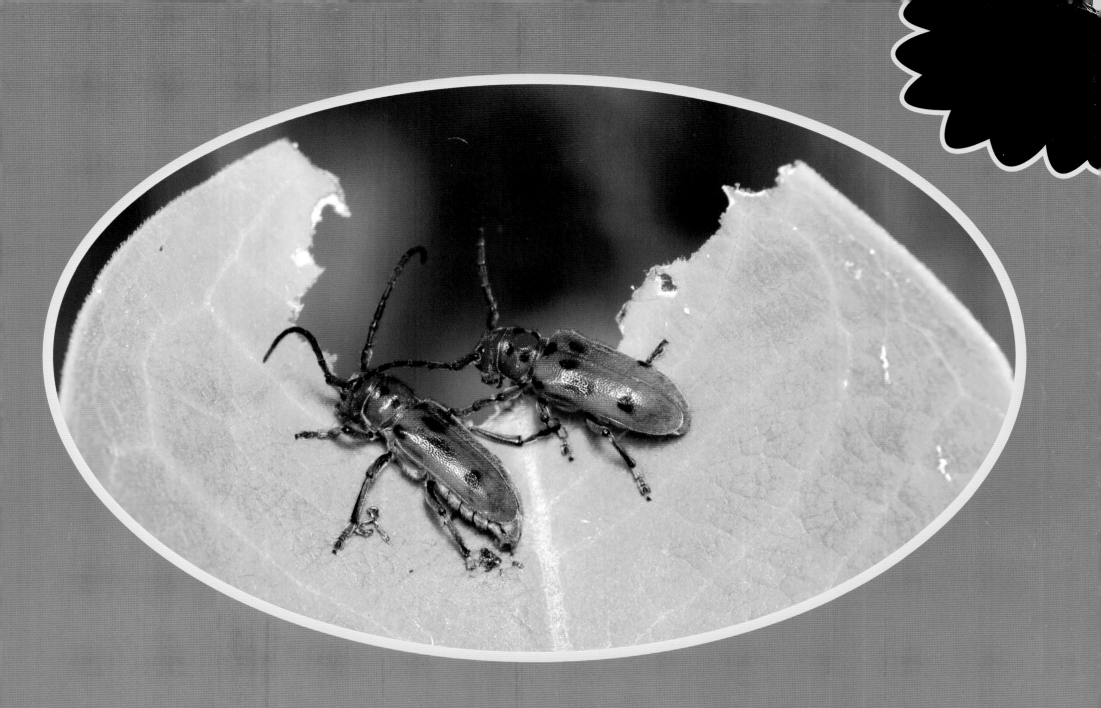

They eat other bugs and plants,
and sometimes even seeds!

Counting beetles

How many red beetles do you see here?
Can you find any that are blue?

Look for beetles all around,
and you could find quite a few!

Answer: two red beetles, one blue beetle.

Did you know?

Beetles are good for your garden because they feed on insects that eat your plants!

Index